T3-BHD-801

Zonal Defending the Italian Way

An in-depth look at the Italian Flat Back Four and Total Team Defending

by

Michele Tossani

Published by
WORLD CLASS COACHING

First published October, 2008 by
WORLD CLASS COACHING 15004 Buena Vista Drive, Leawood, KS 66224
(913) 402-0030

ISBN 9780979994838
Copyright © WORLD CLASS COACHING 2008

All rights reserved. No parts of this publication may be reproduced, stored in a
retrieval system, or transmitted in any form or by any means, electronic, mechanical,
photocopying, recording or otherwise, without prior written permission of the
publisher.

Author - Michele Tossani
Edited by Tom Mura

Front Cover Picture - Marcello Lippi, background, talks to his players during a
training session at the Coverciano grounds.

Published by
WORLD CLASS COACHING

Table of Contents

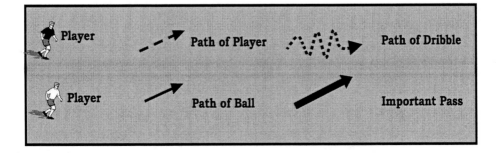

Many coaches talk about the development of the four men in the back line. Although the evolution and the discussions about this topic is never ending, teaching methods and ways to utilize this defensive front are always improving.

Known for their defensive soccer, the Italian Serie A changed their focus in recent years because of the desire to see attractive, attacking soccer by television audiences.

However, strong defensive play remains the mark of Italian soccer. At the last FIFA World Cup, won by Italy, they showed that a solid defense and an average attack is better then a great attack and a so-so defense.

Many Italian coaches prefer to work on the defensive alignments and strategy rather than spending time on offensive schemes.

In Italy coaches have a saying: "Any home is built on the foundation".

It is for this reason that most Italian coaches spend a lot of training time working on their defense.

The four man defensive back line is the most utilized defense system in Italy. Even when playing with three in the back gained more popularity around the world, Italian coaches continued to employ a more traditional defensive system.

The choice of a four man back line depends on the coaches' mentality, players' skills and a study of the opponents, which have begun to play with three forward more often in recent years. Italian coaches feel that they can cover the field better and more easily with four defenders.

The first four teams in the Serie A last season, Internazionale, AS Roma, Juventus and Fiorentina, all utilized a four man defensive back line.

Just a few teams in the Serie A regularly utilized a different system.

Whatever system your team plays, you should study and learn more about the way that Italian coaches organize their teams to be so solid defensively.

Take a look!

Why the Flat Back Four?

Italian soccer is know for its defensive system. The core of this solid defensive system is, clearly, the back line. And, the most common back line in the Italian soccer is the four men back line playing in zones.

Why is this defensive organization is so common in Italy?

There are a number of reasons:

Flexibility

This is one of the motivation for Italian head coaches to use a four man back line as opposed to the three (or five) man defensive front. In fact, with four men on defense you can cover all of the defensive front and you have more chances to turn an attack into a counter attack. With four men on the back line, a team can send one of these men forward, without losing the ability to cover in the back.

Balance

Deploying a formation with four defenders allows for enough cover in all positions. No matter how you line up the midfielders and forwards, with four men in the back you can have an overall balance to the team.

Simplicity

A four men defensive front is a very simple defense to teach and play as all players have played in the system during their careers. The learning curve is faster and coaches don't have to spend a lot of time teach the basics of this system.

The most common system played in recent years in the Serie A is the 4-4-2. Now, starting from this system, many coaches deployed some complex variations of the 4-4-2, such as 4-2-3-1; 4-4-1-1; 4-3-3 or 4-3-2-1. In this book we are going to see how the Italian teams prepare to play this defense for the matches and how they utilize midfielders and forwards to defend as team.

In Italy there exists the perception that the team which has a strong defensive bunch have more chances to bring home the championship so Italian coaches spend a lot of time in pre-season ,as in the regular season, organizing the defense. In this back line, every player is responsible to cover a particular zone of the field.

Defenders Position Depends On
- The ball
- Their teammate
- The opponents

In a four man back line, two players have to cover the central zone and two player have to cover their respective flanks.

Central defenders, central backs or centre-halves play behind the midfield and their primary goal is to be ready to help the keeper, give aide to the flanks and cover the central box to prevent the opposition from scoring. Usually, Italian head coaches like to line up a mixed pair of players: one defender who is stronger physically and taller and more suited to man to man coverage. The second central back is more able to lead the defensive bunch, very strong tactically, sometimes able to go forward leading the offensive action.

Both players have to be focused and committed to their role. If you split the defensive zone in four zones, one for every defender, you can see that each central backs have to cover a zone of about 14 yards.

On the outside of the defense we have the fullbacks. They have mixed duties, having to be capable in the both the defensive and offensive phases of the game. Italian coaches feel that the modern full back has to have speed, tackling skills, stamina to cover the whole field and to attack as a wing. The prototype of the modern Italian full-back was created in the '60s by Giacinto Facchetti. The strongest fullback in the recent era was Paolo Maldini. Recent top Italian models to play the role are Gianluca Zambrotta and Christian Panucci.

If you split the defensive zone in four zones, one for every defender, you can see that each fullbacks have to cover a zone of about 185 yards. So you understand as the fullbacks have a bigger zone to cover then central backs.

Arrigo Sacchi, the architect of the great Milan team, created a new version of 4-4-2 on the late 80s.

A good defense has to have players with some needed prerequisites.

They are:
- Covering Space
- Slowing the Attack
- Compactness
- Balance
- Control and Patients

Covering Space
Players have to be arranged on the field to limit the space for the opponents.

Slowing the Attack
This means that the defensive players have to able to slow the game in order to contain the opponents.

Compactness
Defenders have to be compact to form an united front behind the ball.

Balance
In every situation, defenders have to cover the back side of the defensive line. This is a key principle: in every situation, a player has to place himself between the opponent with the ball and his own goal. And his teammates have to place themselves in order to give cover to the man placed between himself and the closer teammate.

Every player on this type of defense has to see the ball, his own goal and the opponent placed in his own zone.

Remember: the more a player has to cover his own zone the less he can mark the opponent; likewise, the more a player has to closely mark his opponent the less he can cover his zone.

In Italy, the tendency (but not the rule...) is to cover more, far from your own goal and to mark more tightly close to the goal.

Control and Patients
Attention and concentration are the keys to be a good defender: there is no panic and no hurry to tackle in this position. A mistake in this zone of the field could cost too much.

Also, defenders have to think as a group. In the zonal defense, every defender is responsible for his zone and for the close to him zones close to him.

Also, defenders are the first attackers when they get the ball. By the same token, strikers are the first defenders when the ball is lost. This is an important concept in all defending but especially in Italy. In fact, Italian coaches train their forwards to be in position when the team defends so they can be the first foothold in the next offensive play. Also, when the ball is up top, coaches demand that their defenders be organized to prevent a counterattack.

The Back and Midfield Lines

Defensive Back Line

A good defender must close distance the between the defensive and midfield lines. They must move their feet quickly always reacting to the position of the ball. They must also know when to stay and mark the attacker and when to cover. They must also know when to tackle and when avoid tackling.

What to look for:

What are the things the Italian coaches are looking for?

- Gaps between players
- Reaction and movements
- Organization
- The defense knows when to stretch to cover a larger space
- Players select the correct diagonals
- The players slide in relation to the position of the ball

The most important tactical movement to teach to the players is the defensive diagonal.

Obviously, this is the key to playing well with a defensive back four. A good defensive diagonal means that the players can cover the whole defensive side. A bad defensive diagonal could easily generate issues and holes in the defensive unit.

A Long Diagonal

A Short Diagonal

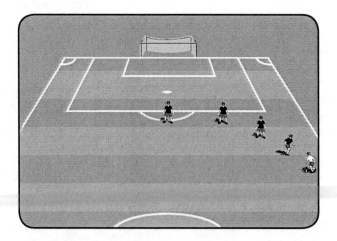

In a long diagonal the gap between the players is greater, notably between the back on the strong side and the central back on the same side. Remember, the strong side is the part of the field where the opponent that has the ball is located. The weak side is the side away from the ball.

In the systems where you have players with the assignment to come back to help the defensive line, as in the 4-4-2 or in the 3-5-2 patterns, defensive diagonal can be closer, because you have a player ready to come back.

In systems where you don't have a player with these assignments, as in some 4-4-2 or in the 4-3-3, the defensive diagonal have to be larger, because you don't have a player ready to become the a fifth defender.

In this case, the responsibility to cover behind the defender on the strong side will be the duty of a midfielder.

Against the central attacks, we play a central diagonal, or defensive "pyramid".

As you can see, one defender goes out while the other three defenders cover their zone. The two defenders closer to the pressuring player have to cover.

Two of the harder problems to solve for a team in the defensive phase:
- Deny a central attacking midfielder
- How to behave against a pass-back in a very deep zone of the field

What are the tactical elements used by the Italian Serie A coaches to solve these problems?

Central Attacking Midfielder

For the most part of the Italian coaches like to cover the central offensive midfielder with the own central midfielders.

The midfield line slides creating one or two lines of coverage in the way to mark the attacking midfielder.

If the attacking midfielder goes over this line, it's the duty of the defenders to cover him.

Otherwise, if the central attacking midfielder remains between the two lines, it's the assignment of holding midfielder to cover him.

Vice versa, where do Italian coaches move their own central attacking midfielder defensively?

They usually use the central attacking midfielder to attack the opponent's central midfielder who is more suited to starting the action.

Reacting to a Pass Back

This is one of the hardest situations to handle. In fact, often a player runs to the end of the field and, instead of sending the ball into the box, they pass back for an upcoming team mate. In this situation, some teams opt to hold firm, playing a zone or a man-to-man coverage in the box.

 © WORLD CLASS COACHING

Some Italian coaches like to push the defensive line up, to keep the team "short" or compact, and to take away depth from the opponents.

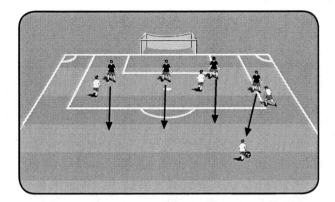

Many Italian head coaches like to switch from a zone defense to a man-to-man coverage when the ball is in a crossing zone far up the field.

The question is: where to try to force the opponent with the ball?

There are two schools of thought between the Italian coaches. For the most part they like to address the opponent with the ball at the outside, because it's a less dangerous zone (less space to attack, less field to see) and because of this, the team has more time to organize an efficient defense.

Other coaches like to force the opponent inside: that happens when they have a strong holding midfielder able to double team or a weak defense against headers; a pattern with more then one holding midfielders, such as in some 4-3-3 systems

Modern Defensive Systems

A brief story

The first head coach to play an effective, modern, defensive zone, was the Swedish Nils Liedholm, with AC Milan and then AS Roma.

His teams was known for the off-side trap (done not with the advancing of the defense but with the stop of the defensive line stopping when the forwards has gone over the line).

Another coach well known in Italy for his defensive zonal approach was another Swedish coach: Sven-Goran Erickson, boss of Florentina, AS Roma, and Lazio before he was the England National Team coach.

Two of the best defensive systems the 2007-8 season were, without a doubt, the flat four men back lines installed by Arrigo Sacchi and Fabio Capello.

Sacchi also used his 4-4-2 with the Italian National Team which finished second in the 1994 FIFA World Cup.

Capello used this system with AC Milan, Juventus and Real Madrid.

At Milan and Real Madrid he played a particular version of 4-4-2, employing a midfield with a defensive wing opposites to an offensive wing.

At Milan, the offensive wing was Montenegrin Dejan Savicevic, former player of European Champions Red Star Beograd.

Sometimes, Capello lined up a second offensive wing with the former Italian National Team head coach Roberto Donadoni. To put Savicevic on the field and a forward not able physically to come back to defend such as Roberto Baggio (you could see him in the USA World Cup of 1994), Capello played with two holding midfielders as Demetrio Albertini and French National Team member Marcel Desailly, a former defender switched in the middle of the field.

At Madrid, Capello played in a similar way using Raùl as a winger.

Having these offensive players as wide players, in a 4-4-2, you have to display long diagonals, because these players would be less able to come back into the defensive line.

The Juventus of Macello Lippi also played a 4-4-2 system, winning the championship and Champions league.

And, while at Juventus, Fabio Capello also utilized a 4-4-2 system, with two offensive flankers in German Camoranesi and Pavel Nedved, mixed with two anchor midfielders such as Patrick Vieira and Brazilian Emerson.

Fabio Capello is the prototype of the traditional Italian head coach since he likes to teach the defensive phase before the offensive phase.

His team was well-known and highly-regarded as a 'pillbox', meaning that it was hard to score against them.

Now that we've discussed the history of Italian teams and coaches that have played with a four man back line defense, it's time to take a look a the modern defensive systems employed by Italian coaches.

FC Inter

The team that won three championships in a row, under coach Roberto Mancini showed some different types of systems but all those systems had a common factor: the use of a flat back four defense.

With the 4-4-2 pattern, Inter played with two defensive bunches of four men, building a wall of eight men in front of the box.

This box was able to slide to the left or to the right in relation to the ball position.

The key to Inter's play with this system, was the balance of the two forwards ready to slide to have a function as support for a quick counter attack.

Defence to attack...

As you can see in the next diagram, when the ball is in an advanced area of the field, the midfielders play a defensive diagonal where the wing opposite to the ball is aligned with the wing on the strong side.

When the ball is over the first defensive line, on the wide side, the central midfielder opposite to the ball is ready to insert himself into the defensive bunch.

Having speed up top from players like Ibrahimovic or David Suazo, Inter can try to recover the ball at a lower level of the field. This means that the forwards come back to win the ball as in ice hockey's collapsing defense.

Against long balls, the Inter defends with a player who goes toward the ball and with the other three defenders who build a deeper line of coverage.

This solution is to prevent a ball over the defensive line by having defenders that play in front of the ball, in an easier situation to defend.

Holding midfielders stay close to the defenders to capture the "second" balls.

The forwards form the first line of pressure by being active in the defensive phase of the game.

They pressure the opposite defensive line and try to:
- stop easy ball circulation by the opposing team;
- force the opponents to send long balls that are easy to defend by tall defenders as are those usually employed by Inter.

This pressing action, by the way, isn't too strong, so that forwards don't spend a lot of energy chasing their opponents.

Having the forwards pressure the opponents defenders isn't done just to be ready for the counter attack but also to have 11 men under the line of the ball. So players at Inter are really a team, defending all together.

A trait of Mancini's Inter was the speed of their transition phase. When the ball is lost, the whole team try to jump back quickly to deploy a large number of players between the ball and the own keeper.

When Inter played with a 4-3-1-2, a 4-4-2 diamond formation, the attacking midfielder didn't have a lot of responsibilities in the defensive phase, having restricted their assignments to slide towards the zone that the ball is in.

With this system, Mancini ask the three midfielders to cover the middle of the field, designing a seven man wall (defenders+midfielders).

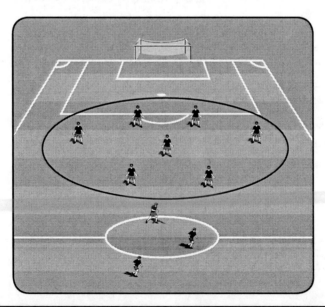

AC Milan

Another variation of the 4-4-2, commonly described as the 'Christmas Tree' formation, was employed recently by AC Milan. The team was trained by Carlo Ancelotti, former assistant of Arrigo Sacchi with the National Team and former head coach of Juventus.

In this system, the team is lined up as in the diamond 4-3-1-2 pattern, but the offensive triangle is reversed so you have two attacking midfielders to play between the "enemy lines" so there are a total of four lines of players: four defenders; three middle midfielders; two attacking midfielders; one forward.

In the defensive phase, you have a large central concentration of player that allows the team to create a double wall of three + two players in the middle to guard the defensive block.

The defensive key to the Milan system is the capacity to connect the two attacking midfielders with the three midfielders, building a dam against attacks.

As pointed out by Ancelotti, this system has a difficult time defending a large part of the field if the ball is switched from one side to the other, because there is just one player (a fullback) to cover the flank on each side.

How is the Christmas Tree formation utilized by the Italian coach to defend as team?

In this defensive pattern: the team has three retaining walls with the attacking midfielders; with the holding midfielders; with the defenders.

That said, AC Milan defends this way:

With the ball on the flank, at an high level of the field, the first defense is the assignment of the attacking midfielder.

With the ball on the flank in the central area of the field, the interior midfielders have the assignment to pressure the opponent with the ball while the attacking midfielder on the strong side will go to cover the opponents midfielder as to prevent an combination play.

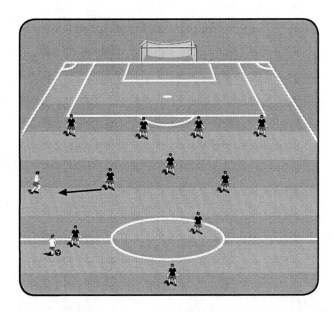

With the ball near the defending zone, it is the fullback's job to pressure.

With the ball in a central area of the field, the AC Milan's defensive system depends on the opponents's formation:

- Against a 4-4-2, Ancelotti asks his attacking midfielders to cover the opposing central midfielders, while the lone forward slides along the offensive front.

Against a three men back line team, Ancelotti ask his offensive trio to pressure the defenders.

If the ball goes from a defender to the flanker, the interior midfielder has the assignment to cover him, while the attacking midfielder near the ball goes to contain the midfielder closest to the ball. The opposite attacking midfielder slides to the central area of the field.

As general rule, when the team lost the ball on the offensive side of the field, Ancelotti asked his team to drop back in order to reorganize the defensive front, before they attack the ball again.

For the AC Milan coach, in this situation, the key to prevent a counter-attack is to rebuild the defense rather than quickly attack the ball in a reckless way.

In order to give the team time to rebuild it is very important that the player closest to the ball move to pressure it. His movement towards the ball gives the rest of the team time to collapse and rebuild the defense.

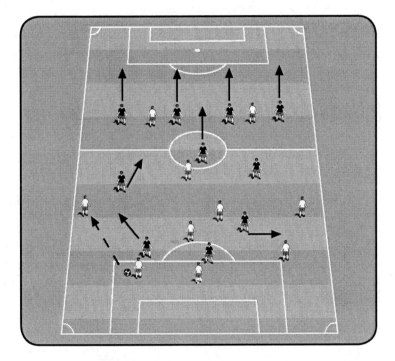

FC Juventus

Claudio Ranieri returned to the Italian Serie A with FC Juventus, the most well-known team in Italian soccer, having previously served as the head coach for Florentina, Parma, Chelsea and Valencia.

Ranieri employs a multiple pattern system: he does not have a favorite system. Instead he likes to change his formation depending on the team's abilities and the "battle array" of the opponents.

Ranieri is wiling to switch the players positions or patterns during the match and from one match to another.

For example: in the 2007/08 season, Ranieri ran a three forwards formation against AS Roma, lining up National Team member Vincenzo Iaquinta, standout captain Alessandro Del Piero and French International David Trezeguet all together. The score was a brilliant 1-1 away tie.

On the return match, Ranieri lined up Czech Pavel Nedved as left wing; forward Vincenzo Iaquinta as right wing; Alessandro Del Piero and David Trezeguet as forwards. Juventus won 1-0.

Also, in Juventus' 2-1 away win against FC Inter, Ranieri ran a classic 4-4-2 pattern with two pure wingers in Pavel Nedved and former Bayern Munich Hasan Salihamidzic, and with two forwards up top.

Ranieri has one constant in all of his teams and that is the usage of a flat back four in the defensive line.

The most utilized pattern by Ranieri was the 4-4-2 alignment. A key element of the Juventus' defensive system is the usage of the off-side trap.

While most of the Italian teams utilize a soccer version of hockey's collapsing defense, Juventus prefers to trap the opponents in off-side positions.

This method depends on:
- The coach's willingness to play offensively so that the team play at a very high level of the field
- The style of play of Juventus' opponents, which often play defensively against this great squad
- The presence of central back Nicola Legrottaglie, who is a defensive leader very capable of leading his team

In general, when it's possible to do it, Ranieri asks his team to press very high. All the players, depending on their skills, have to cooperate in the defensive phase. The type of pressing action (high, medium, low) also depends on the opponents' abilities.

Covering the spaces is important in the Juventus' system.

Juventus, as with any other Italian team, is ready to switch quickly from defensive action to a count-attack.

When the team is attacking, Juventus' defenders don't remain passives, they continue to mark the opponent forwards which remain in their defensive zone.

AC Fiorentina

One of the strongest teams in the 2007-8 season was, without doubt, AC Fiorentina, coach by Cesare Prandelli. The team's system is the 4-3-3.

The flat four man defensive back line is the foundation of the Fiorentina pattern. For the Fiorentina's coach, the defense has to be able to work alone.

This means that Fiorentina plays long diagonals, without a midfielder sliding back to become the fifth defensive man.

That said, you must have a very strong defense that is well organized to play in this way.

In the defensive phase, the wingers have to come inside, to form united central front.

This is mainly true for the offensive left winger, which was, in the 2007-8 campaign, the standout Rumanian Adrian Mutu.

The former Inter, Chelsea and Juventus player didn't have a defensive attitude, so they gave him very few defensive assignments.

Prandelli didn't ask him to come back too much, so he asked the right wing to slide back, forming a 4-4-2 formation when the ball was lost.

Mutu had to come back just to middle of the field, covering the central zone but, above all, being ready for an eventual counter attack.

On the flanks, the interior midfielders have the assignments to slide laterally as to help the fullbacks.

Fiorentina's defense play with a single line of coverage.

The defensive line is able to keep the squad "short" on the field, stepping up or collapsing depending on the situation.

AS Roma

The AS Roma was another force in the Serie A the latest two seasons.

The coach is Luciano Spalletti.

As with Prandelli, Spalletti is one of the representatives of Italy's nouvelle vague head coaches.

Roma runs a 4-2-3-1 pattern.

Roma plays with two different types of wingers: one more offensive and one more defensive.

So, in the defensive phase, the attacking midfielder and the most offensive wing come back in the midfield, while the more offensive wing has less defensive duties.

The attacking midfielder has the primary responsibility to oppose the opponent's midfielder.

The two or three players that remain on the offensive side of the field, if the defensive wing delays his run back, the team breaks into two parts, one offensive and one defensive.

That leaves just six men on the defensive side of the ball but provides many supporting players for the counter attack.

So, in Roma's pattern we have some risks on defense to gain more opportunities on offense.

This comes from the offensive mentality of the head coach, Luciano Spalletti, one of the offensive gurus of Italian soccer.

One of the defensive keys to Roma's play is the presence of super midfielder Daniele De Rossi. He is Italian soccer's greatest holding midfielder.

He aides the defensive line providing help in front of the defensive back four.

He comes back into the defensive back four when the ball is on the flanks because his heading skills bring much needed help to the AS Roma defense.

This is a very important detail, because with the fullback gone, De Rossi gives Roma's back line the chance to remain a four man line.

Atalanta BC

Another Italian nouvelle vague coach is Luigi Del Neri. Despite his age, 58 years old, he's a recent addition to the Italian Serie A.

He was the creator of the "Chievo Miracle", the adventure of a neighborhood's team drawn into UEFA Cup.

He was the coach who reintroduced the utilization of the off-side trap as a defensive weapon for Atalanta BC.

His defensive approach is very simple and very complex in the same breath: defense has to be able to work alone. There is rarely help from wings and no help from the holding midfielder in terms of dropping into the back line.

His pattern is a 4-4-2 with two offensive wings and two forwards up top. His defense plays with a single line of coverage; allowing them to force the opponents off-side often.

When a wing is beaten, in the defensive phase, the holding midfielder has the assignment to slide sideways in order to pressure the opponent with the ball.

That happens if the fullback has to mark an opponent in his zone. Otherwise, with no opponent in his zone, the fullback moves forward in the way to help the midfielder and to double the opponent.

The first duty of the Del Neri's defensive phase is to close the centre of the field. The coach thinks that the centre is the most dangerous zone to cover, because a player with the ball in this zone can see the goal and the whole field, while on the flanks, his vision and playing solutions are reduced.

The holding midfielders in Del Neri's teams play more to head off the ball then to clearly confront the opponents in one-on-one situations; they have to cover the spaces more than clash with the attackers.

His central midfielders are used as offensive players. In counter attacking situations, and with a fullback jumped forwards, three defenders remain back. They have to slide towards the ball running off back to delay the opponents play and allowing teammates to come back and help.

The opponent's central attacking midfielder is covered by the defense: if he gets the ball far from the box, one defender comes out from the defensive line to cover him, while the other three defenders step back.

If the central attacking forward gets the ball near the box, one defender comes out to cover him while the other three stop themselves and hold at the top of the box.

Another feature of this version of the 4-4-2 is the work of the forwards on the defensive phase.

Del Neri doesn't like to see forwards chasing opponents so he prefers to use them just to cover the opponents' defensive line as a way to block an easy build up. Without that responsibility the forwards don't spend as much energy and are able to save it for attacking situations.

That's the same for the wings. When a player is beaten by the opponent with the ball, he remains up for the counter attack with the forwards.

National Teams - Italy's National Team

The pattern most used by the Italian National Team in the qualifying tournament for the 2006 FIFA World Cup was the 4-3-1-2, or diamond midfield system.

The coach was Marcello Lippi, former boss of Juventus and Inter. The road to the Germany 2006 World Cup was defined by the competition between Alessandro Del Piero and Francesco Totti for the attacking midfielder starting role. So, the head coach choose to run two different line up's depending on the presence of Del Piero or Totti in the starting lineup.

With Del Piero in the starting eleven, being more of a forward than a pure offensive midfielder, Lippi lined up his formation as a 4-3-3 pattern.

Del Piero was the left wing offensive midfielder. In the defensive phase, Del Piero had the assignment to contain the opponents' right fullback. One of the forward's had the duty to come back to help the midfield, while the right interior midfielder had to cover up the right side.

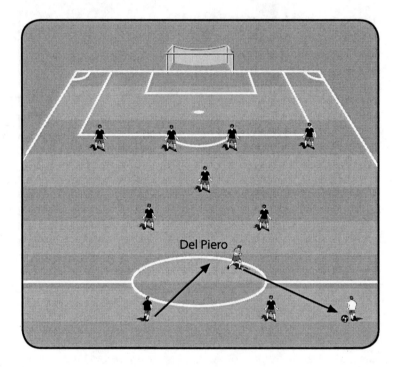

With Totti (grey player) as a starter, being him less suited to cover and to track the opponents, Lippi opted to make a forward slide to the opposite fullback, to cover him or to avoid a pass back (if the forward was late…) while the other forward comes back in the middle and Totti remained up for the counter attack.

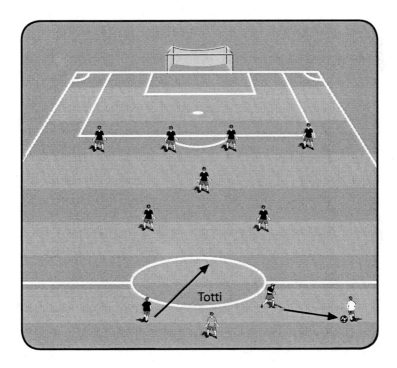

Italian Under-21 National Team

The Italian U-21 team that won the European U-21 Championship in 2004 and won the bronze medal at the 2000 Summer Olympic Games, was coached by former 1982 FIFA World Cup Champion Claudio Gentile.

Gentile installed a mixed defensive system, with the contemporary presence of a zone as well as man-to-man coverage.

On three-fourths of field, the defensive back four switched from a total zone defense to a zone defense for the fullbacks and a man-to-man coverage for the centre backs.

Against two forwards, the centre backs mark the opponents one-on-one, with the fullbacks ready to slide toward the centre to give support.

Against three forwards, the fullbacks have the assignment to contain the opposing wings, while the central halves swap to control the lone forward playing as the old style duo of stopper and sweeper.

Interview
with
Nicola Legrottaglie

Before introducing the most used Italian drills to train the defensive phase in the Serie A, I'd like to share an exclusive interview with the Juventus central back Nicola Legrottaglie.

He speaks about the Juventus way and about the differences between his current head coach and his former boss, Del Neri.

Special thanks to him and to his official fan club for this interview.

Juventus plays with a very high defensive line, such as Del Neri's Chievo done. What are the differences between the two teams?

Defensive systems are different. It's not the same playbook. At Chievo, the defensive back four was more "brave". At Chievo, we played the off-side trap frequently. At Juventus, we don't utilize the off-side trap. We play high so the defensive line is too high to trap. Playing 20 yards forward, we give more scoring chances to our forwards because the distance between them and the goal is shorter.

How did the midfield of Del Neri's play?

The Chievo midfield did the same movements as the defensive back line. That's important. To have a strong defense, you need to have a covering midfield.

Was there a difference in the way you reacted to an attacker being pressured and one that is running freely?

No, it was the same thing. With an free attacker, the defenders have to rush back. The defender has to be able to understand when there is a dangerous situation; when the opponents can create a scoring chance. The defensive line has to understand it. Sure, it's hard to move up and down the field with the opponents for the whole match. Playing a high defensive line was key to us scoring a lot of goals . Forwards scored so much because we played very high. People think we are in a dangerous position with this high defensive line but I disagree. It's simple to play in front of own box, but try to defend so for the whole match. To repeat, with a high defensive line, forwards have less field to cover to score.

Is there one drill used by Del Neri more than any other for his defense.

The 6 v 4 or 10 v 4. In this way, defensive line is ever under pressure. In my opinion, it's important to stop the work, during the drill, in the way to correct the mistakes. And a key is to see the highlights, (we do it every Wednesday). If you don't see the match, you don't understand your mistakes so there is the possibility to repeat those mistakes.

What about the Juventus defensive line?

It's not the same as at Chevo. There is a different attitude. We work on the defensive line's play but Coach Ranieri trusts the defenders more. It's not as at Chievo, where we were young and inexperienced. By the way, the concepts are the same. At his moment, in Italy, we all play this way. That means work on defensive diagonals, pressure and no player on the ball…

Which are your favorite drills?

I like drill matches. The, 6 v 4, done in the right way, is perfect to train the defensive line.

Training Sessions
and Exercises

In this chapter you will find exercises used by Italian coaches to practice the defensive phase of the game.

The first is a drill used by Arrigo Sacchi when he was the head coach of the National Team that took 2nd place in the 1994 FIFA World Cup.

The whole team is lined up on the field. There are also six sticks of different colors spread around. They are lined up as two wings; one forward; two midfielders; one central back. The coach calls one color and the whole team has to attack him with the right defensive formation; defensive diagonals, the team is compact and covering, etc.

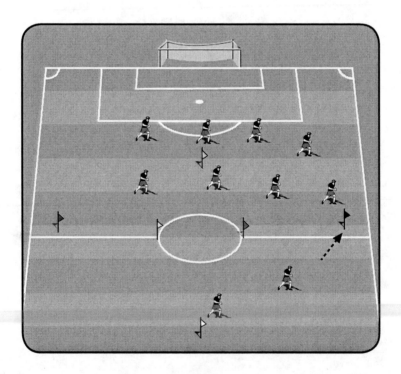

Sacchi and his staff stand at the midfield line. They pass a ball from the left to right and back again. The whole team has to slide, pressuring the opponent with the ball. It's the same drill as before but now the players react to a ball rather than a flag.

The goal of these drills is to look for mistakes in the movement of the team block and of the compactness of the team.

Another Sacchi's drill was to have two teams play; one trying to score and the other to defend the goal. It is played on a reduced field. The defending team is required to press high, training the defense to play compact. The offensive team plays with a maximum of two touches. No one offensive player can start his run from inside the box.

When the defensive team wins the ball, the action is over.

The offensive team can also score one point making 10 consecutive passes.

Tactical work is very important to Italian coaches. The tactical work is usually done in the pre-season training camp. Speaking with many pro coaches, they said that they like to do this work because, after the championship beak, players have the tendency ignore the basics of correct defending.

Tactical Drill 1

On half of a field defenders are lined up. In front of them, there are four sticks, numbered from one to four.

The coach calls a number and the defensive line attacks the corresponding stick, playing with the correct defensive diagonals.

Progression

Sticks are placed all around the field. The coach calls one stick and the defensive line organizes to pressure and cover around that stick, paying attention to the distances, defensive diagonals and all defensive principles.

Tactical Drill 2

The coach moves the ball while the defensive line slides to cover the ball paying special attention to using the correct defensive diagonals.

The defensive back line moves, leaving the weak side open knowing that they can slide over to cover if the ball is switched.

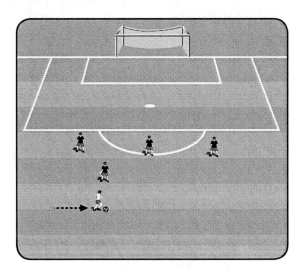

First with one forward in addition to the coach;

Then, with two additional forwards;

Finally, with the coach and three forwards.

As a way to make teaching easier we can split the defensive area into four zones. Each player is responsible for his own zone.

Tactical Drill 3

Introduce forwards as opponents. Interior defenders have to stop the opponents in one-to-one situations. The fullbacks have to show the opponents towards the sideline, as these zones are less dangerous.

If the forward decides to move forward, the defensive back four have to move back to the edge of the box. At that point, the defense will move up to attack the ball. In fact, Italian coaches don't like to defend into the box.

Example of the typical individual defending drills used by Italian coaches.

Technical Defending Drill 1
One attacker and one defender in a 10 X 10 yards playing area.
Each player defends a small goal.

Take a look! The defender has to turn his body in a 45 degree angle in relation to the ball to orientate the opponent's play and movement. Also, the defender has to pay attention to the distance from the opponent. That should be about the length of one arm.

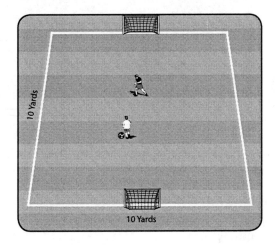

Technical Defending Drill 2
One attacker and one defender in a 10 X 10 yards playing area.
Each player defends the line behind them.

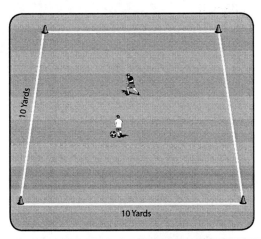

Technical Defending Drill 3

One attacker and one defender in a 25 x 15 yards playing area.
The defender has to defend two goals.

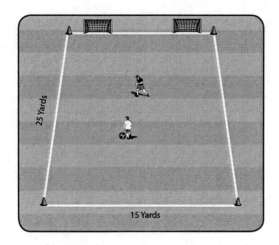

Technical Defending Drill 4

On the same field, one attacker and one defender.
Each player defends two goals.

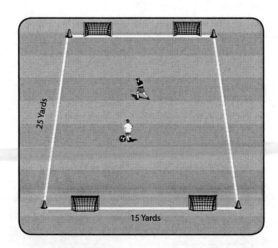

Technical Defending Drill 5

One forward and one defender on the same field with a goal and a keeper on each end. The defender passes the ball to the forward, then goes to defend him and protect his goal.

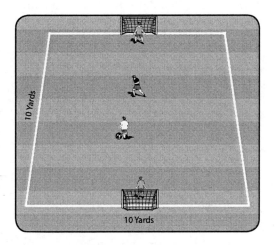

Technical Defending Drill 6

The former Lazio, Inter and AC Milan head coach, Alberto Zaccheroni, believes that this is the key drill to teach zonal play.

On a 10 x 10 yards field, two attackers play against one defender and try to move the ball over the line behind the defender. The lone defender has to move between the opponents, waiting for a mistake or for an off-side to attack the forward with the ball.

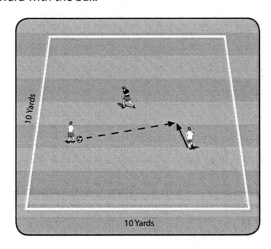

Technical Defending Drill 7
The same drill but now 2 v 2.

With the 2 v 2 drills, Italian coaches start to introduce the concepts of defensive cover, defensive cooperation and defensive diagonals.

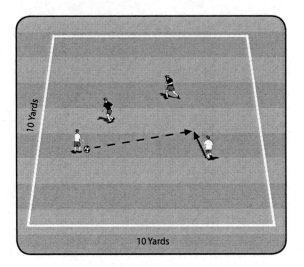

Progression 1
The same exercise but with a third player who plays with the team that has the ball. Each team can score by dribbling across the line.

Progression 2

A more complex 2 v 2 situation is played in a 30 x 30-yard playing area, split into two parts. Defenders have to win the ball and send it to their forward teammates, without moving over the midfield line. In this way, there are always 2 v 2 and counter attack situations.

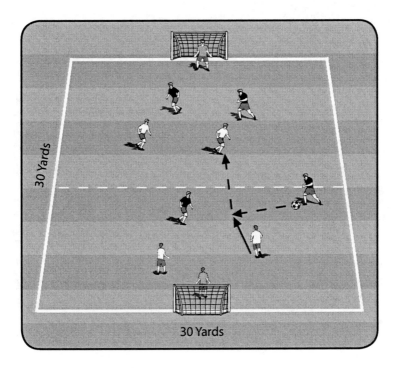

30 Yards

30 Yards

Technical Defending Drill 8
Three attackers and two defenders.

Defenders begin to learn how to play against more attackers than they can cover individually.

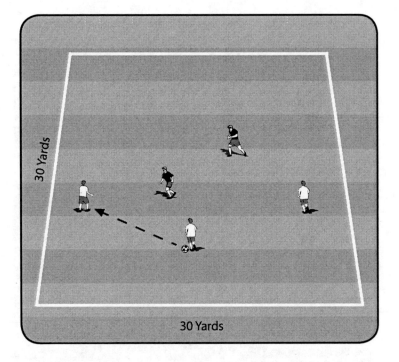

Technical Defending Drill 9

Three attackers try to move the ball past three defenders and across the line.

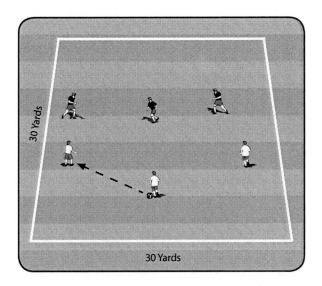

Progression

Three attackers and three defenders work to score.

After that, it's time to introduce the concepts of single and double line of coverages.

Team Defending Drill 1

The defensive back four work to keep four attackers from scoring. There are three way to play:

- 4 v 4 to the line

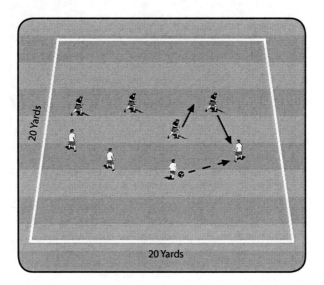

- 4 v 4 to score

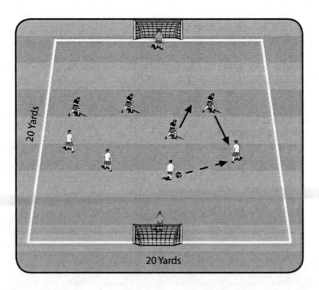

- 4 v 4 keepaway

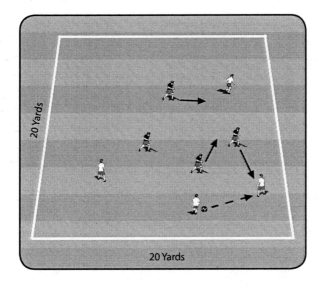

Team Defending Drill 2
Zaccheroni's Drill - 5 v 4

On half of a pitch, Four defenders and one holding midfielder have to defend three small goal placed on the halfway line and try to take the ball into the box to score. This drill trains defenders and forwards simultaneously.

Progression 1 - 10 v 4
This creates a great deal of pressure on the defenders. The attacking team works to score. After each attempt the coach stops the drill and fixes the defensive mistakes.

Team Defending Drill 3

Change the situation adding six offensive players and three defensive players to have a 7 v 10 with more attackers than defenders.

The attacking team tries to score while the defending team attempts to move the ball over a line just the other side of midfield.

Midfielders

Italian coaches like to line up with at least one holding midfielder. At times, in formations with three central midfielders, there are even two defensive midfielders. Italian coaches like to train midfielders in the defensive phase. Here is a look at some exercises involving midfielders.

The same exercise of Team Defending Drill 1 but with four midfielders v four midfielders trying to move the ball across the end line.

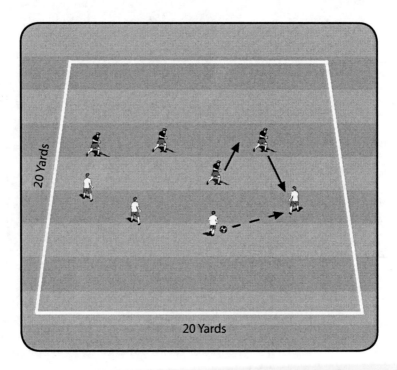

20 Yards

20 Yards

4 v 4 midfielders to score

4 v 4 midfielders with three goals to defend

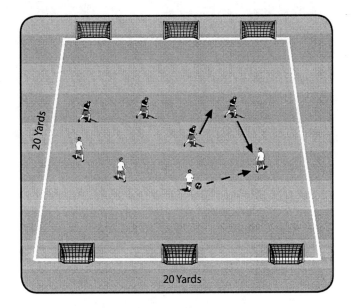

The field is now bigger and split into three zones. In the central zone there are four midfielders that attempt to win the ball.

The outside teams attempt to pass the ball between them, while the midfielders, training their defensive skills and try to intercept the ball without leaving the central zone.

In this a more complex drill each team has a line of defenders and midfielders separated by the other team's midfielders. The goal for each team is to move the ball from their defenders to their midfielders.

The opponent midfielders try to intercept the ball so we have different 8 v 4 situations.

Building Up the Defense from the Back

Two teams: four defenders against six attackers (four midfielders + two forwards). The attackers play to score while the defenders work to prevent it.

Adding Midfielders

Insert two holding midfielders into the defending team and they play against four midfielders and two forwards in a 6 v 6.

Insert two players on the defending team and four on the attacking team to play a 10 v 8. Lengthen the field so that three-fourths is used.

Insert two players on the defending team and play a full 11 v 11 game with goalkeepers.

Playing a Man Down

This works on a tactical solution against the upcoming opponent while playing a man down.

The starting team has nine players while the reserve team is lined up with the formation of the upcoming opponents and has all 10 field players. The starting team tries to defend the open space with the remaining players.

The situation is now reversed with the starting eleven defending the goal and to win the ball to create a counter attack and score in one of the three small goals placed three quarters of the way up the field.

8 v 8

On half a pitch, two teams, play 8 v 8 and try to score in one of two small goals. When the team is on defense their goal is to reduce the time and space for the opponents and defend collectively.

Drill to Train Heading in Defense

Two group of players with the balls stay outside the box. They alternate crosses from the right and left. In the box two pairs of players battle, one to defend the goal and the other to score.

Drill 2 to Train Heading in Defense

Two players send crosses into the box for the defenders to clear with headers. Defenders have to be quick to move into the box to clear the ball before it falls into the box.

Progression 1

Next, do the same drill but add two forwards.

Progression 2

The coach sends the ball towards the forwards. The defenders have to move in front of them to win the ball or move up to leave the attackers offside.

Next, the coach sends another ball to a winger who has to cross for the forwards. The defenders mark their runs and try to clear the ball.

Drill 3 to Train Heading in Defense

This is a fundamental drill to train our defenders how to react when the attackers outnumber the defenders. What do we have to do?

Some Italian coaches decide to mark the forwards closer to the ball, leaving the attacker on the weak side alone.

The coach passes the ball to a winger who crosses into the middle for the three attackers to compete against the two defenders.

6 v 6 Heading Game

Two teams of six play a match with the requirement that the ball must
be passed in the air. This gives the players the opportunity to become
comfortable with competing for balls in the air.

Drills to Teach Defensive Pressing by the Forwards

Drill 1

Two forwards work against the defensive line. The two attackers pressure the defenders and prevent them from moving the ball across the half line.

Drill 2

The same drill, but the forwards play together with four midfielders. The defenders are helped by a holding midfielder.

Drill 3

Eight players form a circle and pass a ball. Their goal is to send the ball through the circle to a teammate. The defending team tries to intercept the ball. The team in the middle receives on one point each time they win the ball. A new group of four players is put in the middle every three minutes.

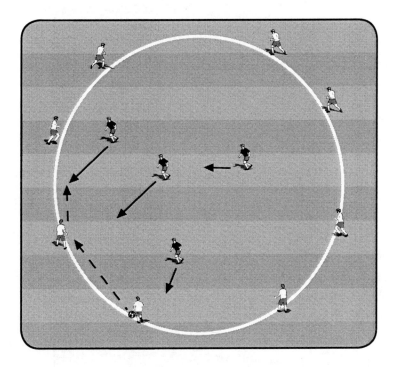

Drill used by Marcello Lippi with Italy for the 2006 World Cup

This is a pressure drill named "Catalunya". Eight eight attacking players with the ball huddled around two defenders in the middle.

The attacking team tries to make passes through the defenders. Change the defenders whenever the ball is one or after the attackers complete eight consecutive passes.

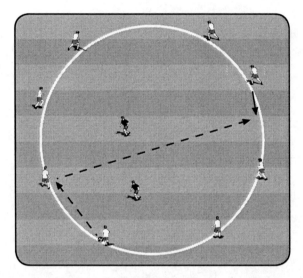

The same drill could be done playing just to intercept the ball so the defenders have with the ball to get out of the middle.

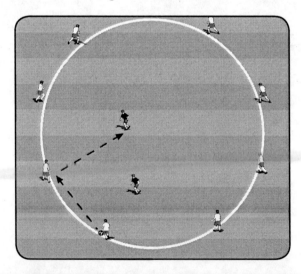

Lippi Drill 2

7 v 7

This is a high intensity game that is played for five minutes. A goal that results from a throw in is worth two points.

Lippi always had more than 14 players in camp with the Italian National Team so he split his roster into three teams. Two teams play and the third rests while stretching off of the field.

Lippi Drill 3

11 v 11

Two teams: one with our formation; the other with the opponent's formation. The goal is to move the ball across the other team's back line.

In a reduced space, three teams play between them. While the third team tries to win the ball. When a team looses the ball, it's turned into the new defending team.

This is a very intense drill. Mix the teams so the fittest players are not all on the same team.

In a reduced space, loaded with sticks, two team of eight players each pass a ball around to hit a stick. The team receives one point for each stick they hit.

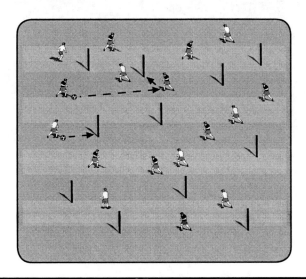

Lippi Drill 4

The field is split into three zones. In an outside zone, two teams play keepaway. If the team that has the ball at the start of the game makes five consecutive passes, it scores one point and sends the ball to the third team for a new match between the third team and the team that lost who move to the other side of the field to try and win the ball.

If they loose the ball, the team that wins the ball send it to the other side of the field. The team that lost the ball has to run to the other side to play against the third team.

Fabio Capello

These are pressing drills used by Fabio Capello when the England head coach was the coach of AC Milan, in the early '90s.

On a 10 x 10 yards field, there are five players outside and two inside. The outside player have one touch. The inside players have to win as many balls as possible. After one minute, there is a change of the two inside player.

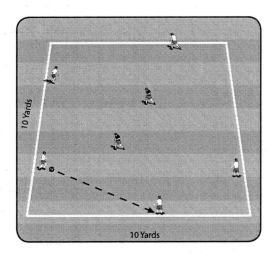

Capello Drill 2

On half a pitch, two team play 7 v 7 without goalkeepers. This very intense drill helps to teach high pressure defending. Both teams try to send the ball over the cross bar to score one point.

Capello Drill 6
10 players v 10 sticks

The team is lined up with our formation to simulated a match against 10 sticks, placed in the upcoming opponent's formation.

The coach calls a stick (numbered from 1 to 10) and the whole team attack them paying attention to the defensive distances and diagonals.

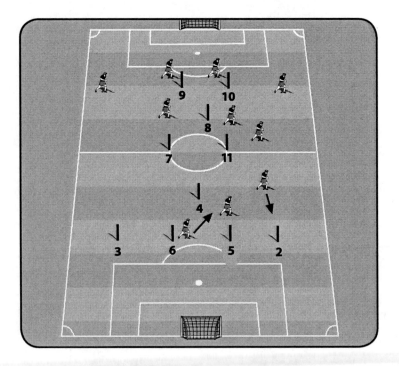

In a reduced space, two team play a 4 v 4 match to the control of the ball.

Adding a neutral player on each end, we train the defense to play against superior numbers.

Drills to Train Defensive Cooperation

The coach moves the ball from the right to the left and back again. The defenders moved to pressure the ball and cover for each other.

Suddenly, the coach moves forward. The defenders have to quickly move backward to cover.

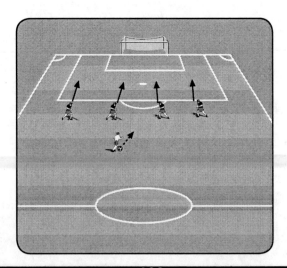

The defense has to "hold", in order to reduce the space the attackers can use. When the coach turns his back to the defenders and comes back to the half line, the defense moves up to make the team more compact.

The coach then moves himself from the right to the left, up and down for a few minutes so the back four can practice moving to cover

The back line is near to the half field line. The coach is just over the line.

The coach kicks the ball towards the box. As the ball is kicked the defenders drop back to keep the ball in front of them and face the attackers.

The Defense has to move quickly. The player positioned in the zone where the ball is played attacks the ball, while the other defenders cover for that player.

The defenders have to be in a position to always be able to see the ball.

Insert three other players as coaches. The four coaches send the ball towards the defensive back four.

The defense has to clear the ball and move up to limit the space for the attackers.

When the ball lands to another coach, the defenders stop themselves and form the line again and be ready to step back all together.

A difficult situation is when the ball is changed from one flank to another. To train this situation four coaches play the ball back and forth while the defensive line slides quickly from one side to the other.

Two defensive lines are organized on either side of four sticks that serve as midfielders. One line moves the ball from side-to-side.

- If they play the ball over the sticks, one defender moves to attack the ball and the others close the space and cover for the player attacking the ball.

- If a player from the group with the ball decides to go past the sticks, the defenders have to collapse. They will attack to the edge of the box (no opponents in the box).

Two Zone Game

In the first zone, four attacking midfielders play against three holding midfielders. The four attacking midfielders move the ball into the offensive zone, where we have three forwards playing against four defenders. The three defensive midfielders try to pressure the ball despite playing a man down. When the ball is under pressure, defensive line rises up, taking away the opportunity for a deep pass to the opponent forwards.

Before the ball is played, the defending team moves up to apply the off side trap.

If the defenders win the ball, they move the ball to their midfielders who attack the other defensive line.

Mario Beretta

This drill, from former Serie A coach Mario Beretta, trains the midfielders to jump back into the defensive back line to restore the defensive balance when a defender has moved to fight for the ball.

Four defenders and two wings against five attacking players, two wings and three midfielders. Attackers move the ball and the defenders slide with the correct defensive diagonals.

When the ball goes to an attacking wing, the defending flanker attacks, while his opposite teammate slides internally cover that area.

If the ball goes to an attacking winger, the defensive line slides, while our wing collapse down to double team while his opposite teammate jumps back to restore the defensive front.

Walter Zenga

These drills were used by the Italian coach who formerly coached the New England Revolution. Zenga played for Inter and the Italian National Team.

This is a drill to reduce the time and space of the opponents and to train his team to play collectively.

Zenga builds a square of about 50 x 40 yards in the middle of the field. Then, lines up the team and put on the field four different sticks at the square's apexes.

The coach calls for the team to move up and down the field and then he calls a stick number and the team has to organize around it quickly.

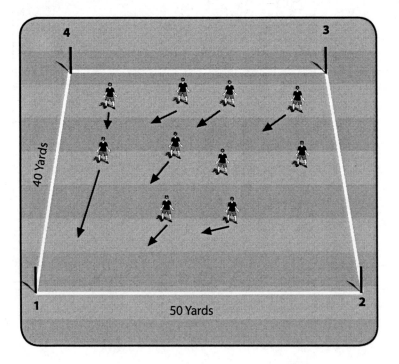

The reduced space forces the team to maintain proper distances.

After this phase, the coach enlarges the square and adds three other sticks in the middle.

Now, there are seven sticks to attack.

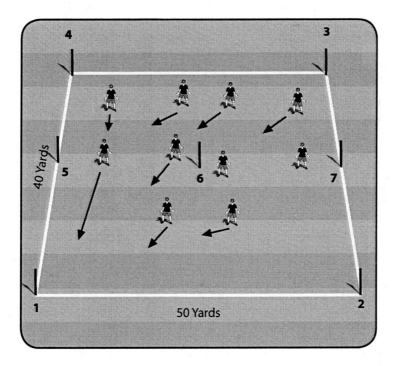

If the opposing team move the ball between the defenders, Zenga wants his team to move up diagonally, to take space, even if it's only a few yards.

When the opponent stops the ball, Zenga's team has to be able to understand when it's time to jump back (when a long ball is probable) or rise again.

He stresses team compactness in his defensive drills.

Pasquale Marino

These drill are used by Udinese's head coach Pasquale Marino to teach the defensive phase of 3-4-3 but can be used with for any formation pattern.

The field is split in three zones.
- In the offensive zone: the four defenders have move out of their zone with the ball in order to create a 5 v 4 situation in the middle
- In the middle: now, in a 5 v 4 situation, the team with the ball tries to move one player with the ball and one player without the ball into the offensive zone

If the play start from the three defenders, they have the objective to go up the middle with the ball. If they fail to do it, then they will play a 3 v 4.

The forwards of either team can't come back into the middle zone to be ready for the counter attack and to accustom the defending team to play with 2 players less.

Four Forwards Attack Three Defenders

One defender is held out and has to be able to recover to help his teammates. The three defenders have to move back toward the edge of the box, to allow their teammate to recover.

11 v 11

The starting team play against a passive reserve team to score. When the goal is scored, the reserve keeper plays a ball to his team. The first team has to be able to recover quickly to get pressure on the ball and a good defensive shape behind the pressuring player.

Modern Soccer Conditioning

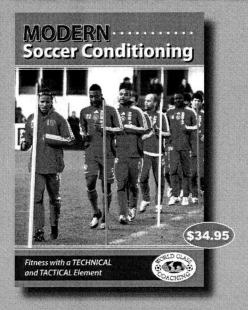

Conditioning or Technique? Are you using valuable time during your training sessions to condition your players with sprints and shuttle runs? Do you have to choose between fitness exercises and working on improving technique or tactics? If so, this is the DVD you have been waiting for.

Now you don't have to choose. This DVD will show you how to integrate conditioning into your regular training sessions while your players have a ball at their feet and they are improving their technique or you are working on team tactics.

Over the past few years giant strides have been made in the area of specialized conditioning for soccer players. Now soccer teams at the highest professional levels utilize this integrated form of "total" soccer training, in order to train more intelligently and efficiently. This DVD shows the following type of workouts... all done with a ball.

Order this DVD and many others from
www.worldclasscoaching.com

Legendary 1v1 Moves

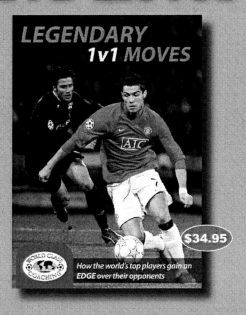

Soccer games are often decided by a series of 1v1 contests all over the field. The world's best players both past and present like Ronaldo, Maradona, Johan Cruyff, Zidane and Ronaldinho, all had "Legendary 1 v 1 Moves" that gave them the EDGE over defenders in 1 v 1 situations. It's these moves that separated them from other players and helped them become the best players in the world.

Now you can take your game to the next level by learning the very same moves used by the world's best players. This DVD will show you 15 Legendary 1 v 1 Moves – Fake Shot, Puskas, Pull Back & Play, Maradona Turn, Rivelino, Swivel Stepover, Scissors, Matthews, Swivel/Swivel, TapNPlay, Stop Hop & Roll, Cruyff Turn, Spin Cruyff, Touch Hop/Scissors, Ronaldinho.

Order this DVD and many others from
www.worldclasscoaching.com